Women's Witticisms

ISBN 1-59931-000-7

First printing • October 2005

Additional copies of this book are
available by mail. For information:

cljdesignsinc@aol.com

P.O. Box 3547
Rancho Santa Fe, CA 92067

Women's Witticisms

Tamara Lafarga Novick

Contents

Acknowledgements

I would like to acknowledge and thank the following people:
my mother for teaching me to love and appreciate life,
my husband for his companionship and care,
and my children for making me a proud and blessed mother.
My gratitude is also extended to
my grandson for bringing pure joy into my life.
A special thanks to Sully, and to all my friends
for their continual support.
It is because of all these people that I was inspired
to create this book.

This book is dedicated to all women,
so that they might be inspired and touched by its contents.

Woman "... the standard general term for the adult human being of the sex distinguished from man..."

~ Webster's New World College Dictionary, Fourth Edition

Being a woman ...

Being a woman

means finding
the balance
between strength
and kindness, patience
and force, femininity
and independence.

- Allison S. Costa (25)

Being a woman

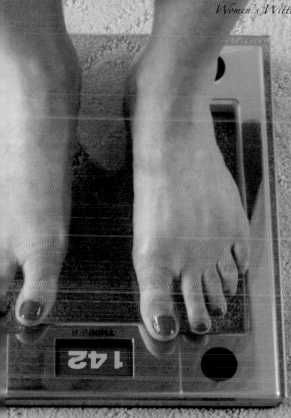

To be comfortable in whatever
skin you are in, be it stretched,
engorged or wrinkled.

– Crystal Miller (24)

line to go to the bathroom... means standing

ne to go to the bathroom... means standing

– Tamara L. Novick (49)

Being a woman

Multi-tasking is a given.

- Shane Lezcano (18)

Being a woman

You fix it, bake it, love it, make it,
discover it and a man gets all the credit.

- Carolyn DeBoer (36)

Being a woman

means dealing with hormonal changes.

– Karen L. Suggs (52)

Being a woman

...arriving at the age where you know and accept yourself.

- Kahloah Dillard (13)

Being a woman

is the ability to play
many roles in a lifetime.
~ Wanda Zwick (77)

Daughter "... a girl or woman as she is related to either or both parents..."

~ Webster's New World College Dictionary, Fourth Edition

Being a daughter...

Being a daughter

Turning out like your mother
whether you like it or not.
A mother's children
are the portraits of herself.

- Suzanne Shetney (70)

Being a daughter

Trying to live up
to your
parents expectations.

- Clara Ruth Novick (80)

Women

Being a daughter

Always knowing that you
have someone on your side.

- Cherie Mull (23)

Being a daughter

Having an ultimate connection
with one human being
that is everlasting.

– Mara Zigman (41)

Being a daughter

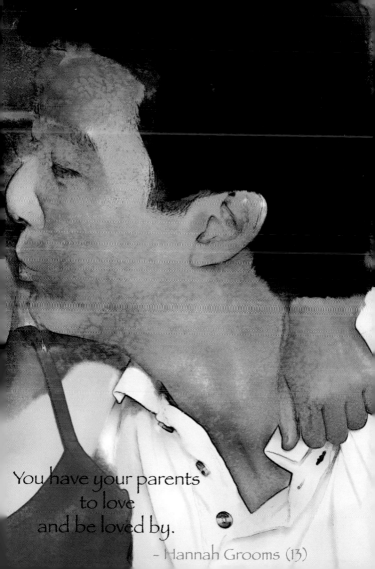

You have your parents
to love
and be loved by.

– Hannah Grooms (13)

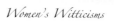

Being a daughter

Learning respect and obedience,
as well as gratitude.

- Tamara L. Novick (19)

Being a daughter

Knowing that someone
out there cares,
not about what
others think of you,
but rather what you
think about yourself.

– Jessica Bashara (13)

Being a daughter

Loving and appreciating
your mother
because of the dreams
she put on hold,
enabling you to become
who you were meant to be.

- Carol Ann Walker Cohen (47)

Sister "... a woman or girl as she is related to the other children of her parents... a close female friend who is like a sister..."

~ Webster's New World College Dictionary, Fourth Edition

Being a sister...

Being a sister

the one who can
comfort and torture the other sibling
most effectively.

- Lia Andrews (27)

*Being
a
sister*

**means
not having to
worry
about
the
small
talk.**

- Cindy Lafarga (46)

Being a sister

Better than a brother.

~ Lisa Lee (40)

Being a sister

Share, share, share.
Share possessions,
share emotions,
share responsibilities.

- Tamara L. Novick (49)

Being a sister

flirting
with your
brother's
friends.

- Molly Miller (14)

Being a sister

an unconditional bond between
siblings to which no one else can relate

- Lynn Marie (48)

Being a sister

letting your sister borrow
your clothes,
even when she does not
let you touch hers.

~ Susana Kidd (28)

Being a sister

someone who understands you
and shares your childhood memories.

- Janice Rosell (35)

Friend "... a person whom one knows well and is
fond of..."

~ Webster's New World College Dictionary, Fourth Edition

Being a friend...

Being a friend

means never being alone.

- Jen Grooms (9)

Being a friend

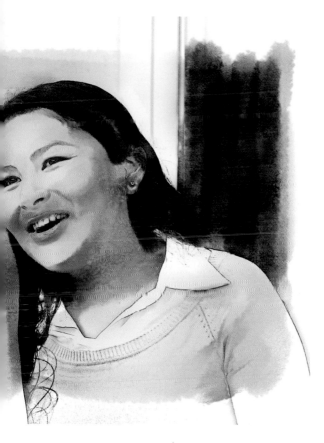

means keeping secrets.

- Sylvia Suggs (18)

Being a friend

means seeing through
the heart, not the eyes.
True friendship isn't
about being there
when it is convenient -
it's about being there
when it's not.

– Erika Evermore (33)

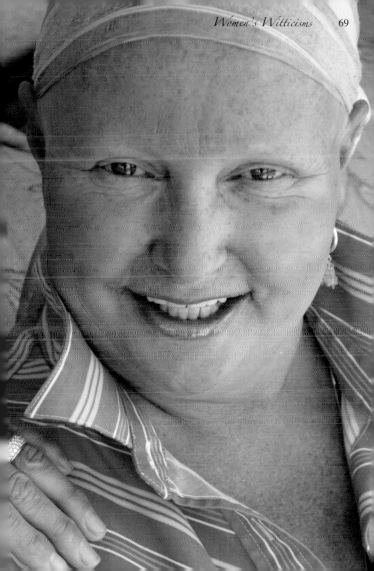

Being a friend

means
trust
and
acceptance.

- Natalie Martin (21)

Being a friend

you can be yourself and you always
have someone with whom
you can talk, cry and laugh.

~ Lauren Lezcano (22)

Being a friend

someone you can confide in
knowing that they genuinely care.

~ Dorothy Clem (84)

Being a friend

being able to pick up where you left off,
no matter how much time has elapsed.

- Aurelia Maciel (52)

Being a friend

being like an angel ~ you don't have
to see them to know they are there.

~ Nancy Bashara (70)

Wife   "... a married woman; specifically a woman in her relationship to her husband..."

~ Webster's New World College Dictionary, Fourth Edition

Being a wife...

Being a wife

loving and living
with your
best friend
for the rest
of your life.
– Laura Maurer (45)

Being a wife

short time single,
long time married.

- Lenore Kessler (78)

Being a wife

in decades past
meant losing
your identity.
Today
it is a partnership,
and a life long
companionship.

- Aurelia Zimbal (91)

Being a wife

depends on
what you get
for a husband.

- Diane Bray (42)

Being a wife

forging through the difficult times,
driven by love
and because
you see the light
at the end of the tunnel.

– Tara Maxfield (25)

Being a wife

Forgiving as a gesture of true love,
compromising when you know
that you are right and striving
to bring out the best in one another.

- Tamara L. Novick (49)

Being a wife

Being his champion and muse.

~ Gayle Grabell (46)

Being a wife

Growing as a person
with your husband
without losing the
person he fell in love with.

~ Elizabeth Kelley (32)

Mother   "... that which gives birth to something, is the origin or source of something, or nurtures in the manner of a mother..."

~ Webster's New World College Dictionary, Fourth Edition

Being a mother...

Being a mother

Being of absolute service
to the development of
another human being,
in which the reward
is in the doing.

– Judith Andrews (53)

Being a mother

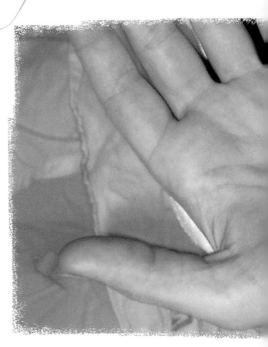

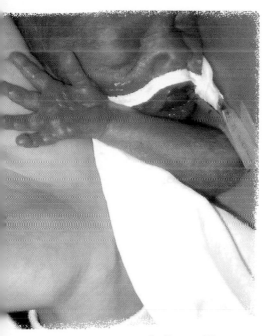

joyfully offering
unconditional love,
sacrifice and time.

- Tamara L. Novick (49)

Being a mother

making responsible choices.
- Darshanda Jackson (22)

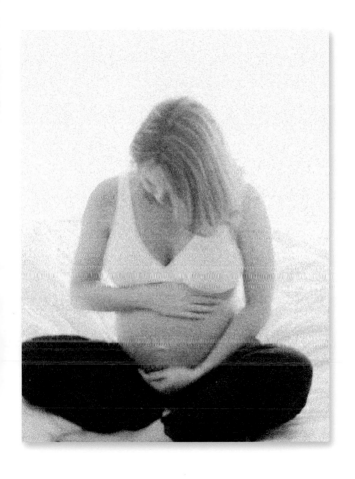

Being a mother

Never getting enough sleep.
Being on call 24/7.

– Sally Guth-Aguilera (49)

Being a mother

being able to slow down
and speed up simultaneously.

-Max's Mom (27)

Being a mother

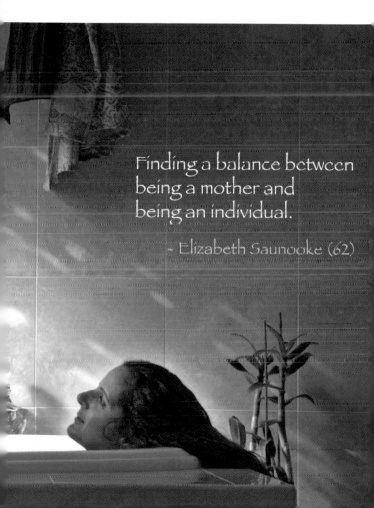

Finding a balance between being a mother and being an individual.

- Elizabeth Saunooke (62)

Being a mother

Teaching your children
right from wrong.
Teaching acceptance,
honesty, compassion
and love.

- Tamara L. Novick (49)

Being a mother

Chauffeuring
and communicating
with the pride of calling
yourself "Mom".

– Lara Pepper (11)

Grandmother "... the mother of ones father or mother: also a term of respectful familiarity to any elderly woman..."

~ Webster's New World College Dictionary, Fourth Edition

Being a grandmother...

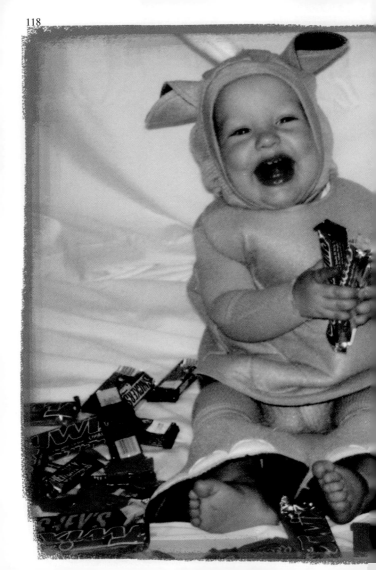

Being a grandmother

Not worrying about
following the rules.

– Alexa Aguilera (16)

Being a grandmother

means being able to act
like a child again.

- John-Kai's Grandmother (70)

Being a grandmother

Giving your children
the two most
precious gifts on earth...
roots and wings.

- Kathy O'Neill (47)

Being a grandmother

means leading
by example.

~ Mary Ann Green (52)

Being a grandmother

The guiding warm light
that accepts a child
as they are without judgment.
Open arms without strings.

– Judy Muller-Cohn, Ph.D. (45)

Being a grandmother

Love, simply love and warmth.

- Marjorie Davis (84)

Being a grandmother

Spoiling your grandchildren.
Experiencing the fun of parenthood
without the responsibility.

~ Porfiria Nocon (81)

Being a grandmother

The legacy and the matriarchal glue
of generations both present and future.

~ Tamara L. Novick (49)

Contributors

Alexa Aguilera	Shane Lezcano
Judith Andrews	Deborah Lindholm
Lia Andrews	Aurelia Maciel
Jessica Bashara	Lynn Marie
Nancy Bashara	Natalie Martin
Diane Bray	Laura Maurer
Dorothy Clem	Tara Maxfield
Allsion S. Costa	Crystal Miller
Marjorie Davis	Molly Miller
Carolyn DeBoer	Max's Mom
Kahloah Dillard	Cherie Mull
Erika Evermore	Judith Muller-Cohn, Ph d
Gayle Grabell	Portiria Nocon
John-Kai's Grandma	Clara Ruth Novick
Mary Ann Green	Kathy O'Naill
Hannah Grooms	Lara Pepper
Jen Grooms	Janice Rosell
Sally Guth-Aguilera	Elizabeth Saunooke
Darshanda Jackson	Suzanne Shetney
Elizabeth Kelley	Karen Suggs
Lenore Kessler	Sylvia Suggs
Susana Kidd	Carol Ann Walker-Cohen
Cindy Lafarga	Mara Zigman
Lisa Lee	Aurelia Zimbal
Lauren Lezcano	Wanda Zwick

Index of Photographs

138

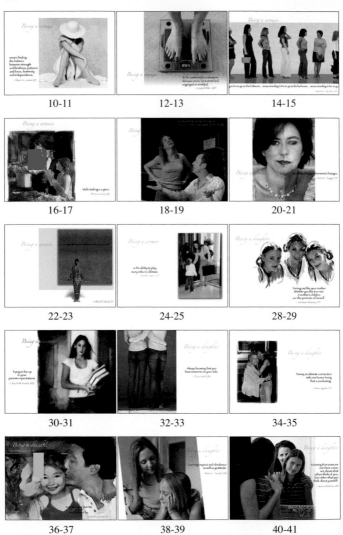

10-11

12-13

14-15

16-17

18-19

20-21

22-23

24-25

28-29

30-31

32-33

34-35

36-37

38-39

40-41

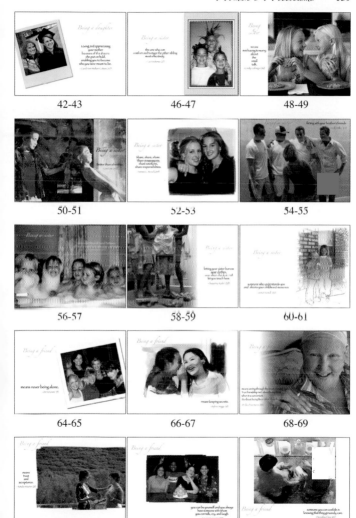

42-43   46-47   48-49

50-51   52-53   54-55

56-57   58-59   60-61

64-65   66-67   68-69

70-71   72-73   74-75

140

110-111   112-113   114-115

118-119   120-121   122-123

124-125   126-127   128-129

130-131   132-133